W9-CFC-586

THE BATTLE OF THE
ALAMO

Janey Levy

The Rosen Publishing Group's

PowerKids Press™

New York

Published in 2009 by The Rosen Publishing Group, Inc.
29 East 21st Street, New York, NY 10010

Book Design: Michael J. Flynn

Photo Credits: Cover © David Gilder/Shutterstock; pp. 3–4 (background), 8–16 (background), 18–25 (background), 27–28 (background), 30–32 (background) © sunnyfrog/Shutterstock; p. 5 © Alexey Stiop/Shutterstock; pp. 6–7 © Aura Castro/Shutterstock; pp. 8–9 (map) © Kenneth V. Pilon/Shutterstock; p. 10 (statue of Austin) http://upload.wikimedia.org/wikipedia/commons/d/db/Austin_statue.jpg; p. 10 (portrait of Austin) © Hulton Archive/Getty Images; p. 13 (Santa Anna) http://upload.wikimedia.org/wikipedia/commons/d/d3/Antonio_Lopez_de_Santa_Anna2.jpg; p. 17 © Stock Montage/Hulton Archive/Getty Images; p. 18 (David Crockett) © John Neagle/The Bridgeman Art Library/Getty Images; pp. 20–21 (battle scene) © MPI/Hulton Archive/Getty Images; p. 22 (coffin) http://upload.wikimedia.org/wikipedia/en/6/68/San_Antonio_067.JPG; p. 25 (battle scene)http://www.tsl.state.tx.us/mcardle/paintings/sanjac-big.html; p. 26 © Andrea Wells/Photographer's Choice/Getty Images; p. 29 (Texas capitol building) © Brandon Seidel/Shutterstock; p. 29 (battle scene) http://www.tsl.state.tx.us/mcardle/paintings/alamo-big.html.

Library of Congress Cataloging-in-Publication Data

Levy, Janey.
  The Battle of the Alamo / Janey Levy.
      p. cm. — (Real life readers)
  Includes index.
  ISBN: 978-1-4358-0167-7
  6-pack ISBN: 978-1-4358-0168-4
  ISBN 978-1-4358-2991-6 (library binding)
  1. Alamo (San Antonio, Tex.)—Siege, 1836—Juvenile literature. 2. Soldiers—Texas—Biography—Juvenile literature. 3. Texas—History—Revolution, 1835-1836—Biography—Juvenile literature. 4. Texas—History—To 1846—Juvenile literature. 5. Frontier and pioneer life—Texas—Juvenile literature. I. Title.
  F390.L485 2009
  976.4'03-dc22

                              2008036889

Manufactured in the United States of America

CONTENTS

A SYMBOL OF COURAGE

"Remember the Alamo!" Have you ever heard that yell? It honors a battle that occurred during Texas's war for independence from Mexico. A small group of men inside a fort called the Alamo fought off an attack by about 4,000 Mexican soldiers. They lost, but their bravery inspired others to continue the fight for freedom. Texas won its independence, and the Alamo became a **symbol** of courage in the struggle for liberty.

The Alamo is in San Antonio, Texas. It was originally a **mission** founded by Spanish priests in 1718. At that time, Spain claimed the area that today forms Mexico and Texas. In 1821, Mexico won its independence from Spain and gained control of Texas. Events over the next few years finally led to the Battle of the Alamo in 1836.

The name of the Alamo may have come from the cottonwood trees that once surrounded it. The Spanish word for cottonwood is *alamo.*

LIFE IN MEXICAN TEXAS

What was life like in Texas under Mexican rule? From the very beginning, there were problems. The new nation's government wasn't concerned with its people's happiness.

The leader of Mexico's **revolution** against Spain was an army officer named Agustín de Iturbide. He made himself president after Mexico won its independence. Then he made himself emperor in 1822! Iturbide used his new power to send people who disagreed with him to prison. He shut down the Mexican congress so he would have complete control of the government. He spent money on himself rather than on Mexico's people. Iturbide's unfair practices were just some of the problems for the people of Texas.

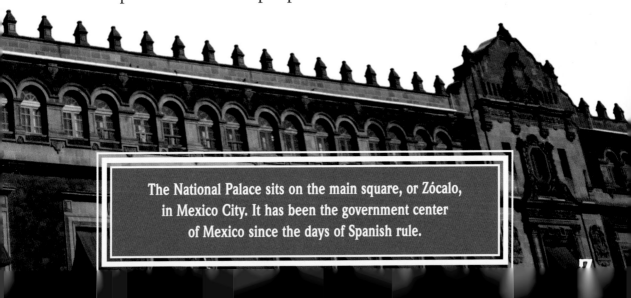

The National Palace sits on the main square, or Zócalo, in Mexico City. It has been the government center of Mexico since the days of Spanish rule.

Texas was a **frontier** region. Although the area is huge, only about 4,000 Mexican settlers lived there. Most Mexicans preferred to live in central Mexico, which they thought had better land for farming. Native Americans occupied most of Texas, and they weren't happy about the settlers living there.

Tens of thousands of Native Americans from many different tribes lived in Texas. Most tribes had been there for centuries. They tried to drive out the Mexican settlers, and there weren't enough settlers to protect all the land claimed by Mexico. To increase the number of settlers and gain better control of the land, the Mexican government decided in 1821 to admit **Anglo** settlers from the United States. This led to even more problems.

This map of Mexico was printed in London, England, in 1821, the year Mexico gained its independence. The words "Great Space of Land unknown" appear over Texas. Few Europeans and Americans knew anything about the region.

Stephen F. Austin

ANGLO SETTLERS BRING MORE CONFLICT

A Missouri businessman named Moses Austin dreamed of establishing a colony in Texas. He died before he could realize his dream, so his son, Stephen F. Austin, set out to accomplish it for him. In 1822, Stephen led the first group of Anglo settlers to Texas. Three hundred families settled on rich farmland in southeastern Texas. Almost immediately, conflict arose between the Anglo settlers and the Mexican government.

Moses Austin had promised the Mexican government that all the settlers would be Catholic, just like Mexicans were. They weren't, though, and they refused to become Catholic. To make matters worse, they refused to speak Spanish and didn't always obey Mexican laws. Not surprisingly, the settlers' actions angered the Mexican government.

This bronze statue of Stephen Austin is on the grounds of Stephen F. Austin State Park in San Felipe, Texas. The park was opened to the public in 1940.

Soon there were more Anglos than Mexicans in Texas. Many Mexicans feared the United States would try to take over Texas. So in 1830, the Mexican government banned more Anglos from settling in Texas and increased its control over the region.

The Anglo settlers complained to the Mexican government in 1833. Their complaints angered Mexico's new president, Antonio López de Santa Anna, and he threw Stephen Austin into prison. In 1834, Santa Anna declared himself **dictator** and put an end to all local governments. The Anglos objected to these actions, which took away many of their rights, and refused to obey Santa Anna. Soon the battle of angry words and actions led to gunshots.

Santa Anna was a vain man who had numerous pictures of himself made. Many show Santa Anna as he appears here—a military leader wearing a dress uniform decorated with medals.

Antonio López de Santa Anna

THE TEXAS REVOLUTION BEGINS

The Texas revolution began in October 1835 at Gonzales, a small Anglo settlement near San Antonio. The Mexican government had given the people there a small cannon so they could protect themselves against attacks by Native Americans. As punishment for the Anglos' refusal to obey Santa Anna, the Mexican army ordered Gonzales to give the cannon back. The townspeople refused, however, and instead fired at the soldiers. Furious, Santa Anna sent more soldiers to San Antonio. He ordered them to take guns away from all Texas Anglos and arrest anyone who opposed him.

The Anglos then took their own actions. Stephen Austin, who had been let out of the Mexican prison in 1834, led a **siege** of the Mexican troops in San Antonio.

The people of Gonzales weren't about to give their cannon to the Mexican soldiers. They made a flag similar to the one shown here and flew it above the town when the Mexican troops came.

Cause 1:
Anglo settlers aren't Catholic, as Moses Austin promised.

Cause 2:
Anglo settlers won't speak Spanish or obey Mexican laws.

Cause 3:
Mexican government increases control over Texas.

Cause 4:
Anglo settlers protest, angering Santa Anna.

Cause 5:
Santa Anna throws Stephen Austin in prison.

Cause 6:
Santa Anna becomes dictator and does away with local governments.

Cause 7:
Anglo settlers refuse to obey Santa Anna.

Cause 8:
Santa Anna sends soldiers to take cannon away from Gonzales.

Effect:
Texas revolution

COME AND TAKE IT

15

In November 1835, Anglo leaders met in what is now the city of Austin to talk about the problems with Mexico. They decided to form their own government and create their own army. They appointed Samuel Houston to lead the army.

A few weeks later—on December 5, 1835—Anglos attacked the Mexican troops in San Antonio. On December 9, the Mexican soldiers **surrendered** and withdrew. About 100 Anglo settlers then took over the Alamo.

Houston knew the Mexican army would try to retake the Alamo. On November 12, 1835, several weeks before leading the attack against the Alamo, Houston had called for **volunteers** to join the settlers there and help them fight.

In this portrait of Samuel Houston, made in the late 1830s, Houston's hand rests on a map of Texas.

Samuel Houston

THE BATTLE OF THE ALAMO

Santa Anna and about 4,000 soldiers reached the Alamo on February 23, 1836, and began a siege. Inside the mission were fewer than 200 soldiers and volunteers, plus some women, children, and slaves. William Barret Travis, a Texas army officer, commanded the soldiers. Famous **frontiersman** James Bowie led the volunteers, who included another famous frontiersman, David Crockett.

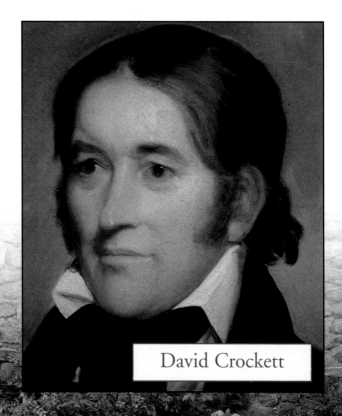

David Crockett

Crockett is popularly known as Davy Crockett. However, he always called himself "David," not "Davy."

On February 24, Travis sent a soldier to Gonzales with a letter pleading for more volunteers and promising that he would "never surrender or retreat." A newspaper printed Travis's letter on March 2. Another printed it on March 5. Hundreds of volunteers answered the appeal, but they didn't reach the Alamo in time.

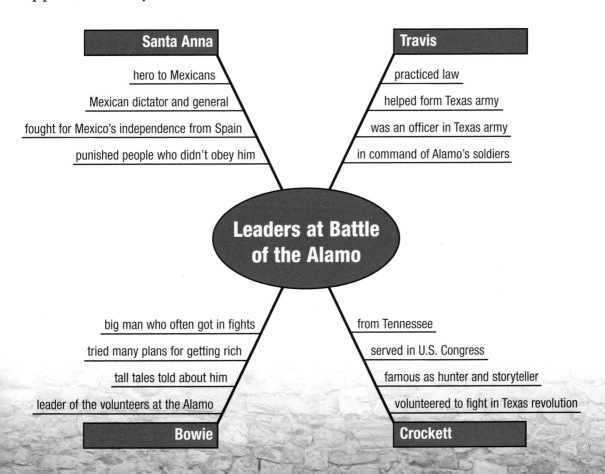

Leaders at Battle of the Alamo

Santa Anna
- hero to Mexicans
- Mexican dictator and general
- fought for Mexico's independence from Spain
- punished people who didn't obey him

Travis
- practiced law
- helped form Texas army
- was an officer in Texas army
- in command of Alamo's soldiers

Bowie
- big man who often got in fights
- tried many plans for getting rich
- tall tales told about him
- leader of the volunteers at the Alamo

Crockett
- from Tennessee
- served in U.S. Congress
- famous as hunter and storyteller
- volunteered to fight in Texas revolution

For 13 days, the Mexican soldiers shot at the Alamo, and the Alamo **defenders** shot back. By March 5, 1836, though, the defenders were running low on **ammunition** and weren't firing back. Santa Anna knew it was time to attack. The assault began around 5:00 A.M. on March 6.

The Alamo defenders fought bravely from the tops of the walls surrounding the mission. However, there were too few of them, and soon the Mexican soldiers had succeeded in climbing the walls.

Travis was one of the first to die. The remaining defenders fought until they ran out of ammunition. Then they used their rifles as clubs and kept fighting.

In this painting—made in 1903 by Robert Jenkins Onderdonk—David Crockett (center) is depicted using his rifle as a club to fight off Mexican soldiers. Today, this painting hangs in the governor's mansion in Austin, Texas.

The battle lasted less than an hour and a half. When it was over, Mexico had retaken the Alamo. All the defenders died. Most historians believe all of them died during the battle. Some think that a few, including Crockett, **survived** but were killed immediately afterward on orders from Santa Anna.

Not everyone inside the Alamo died. Women, children, and slaves survived. Santa Anna gave each of them a blanket and $2.00 and set them free. They spread news of the battle.

The Mexican victory at the Alamo was a terrible blow to the Texas revolution. The Mexican army felt certain they would crush the revolution. However, that isn't what happened.

Some historians believe this marble box—kept at the San Fernando Cathedral in San Antonio, Texas—contains the remains of David Crockett, William Travis, and James Bowie.

TEXAS WINS ITS INDEPENDENCE

While the Alamo was under siege, representatives from all fifty-four Anglo settlements met and signed the Texas Declaration of Independence. The declaration stated Texas was an independent republic, but Texas still had to win the war.

On March 27, the Mexican army surprised 500 Texas soldiers at Goliad. The soldiers surrendered immediately, but Santa Anna still had them all killed.

Everything changed at the Battle of San Jacinto. Soldiers led by Sam Houston caught up with the Mexican army. Shouting "Remember the Alamo!" and "Remember Goliad!" they attacked the Mexican troops while they slept. When the battle ended 18 minutes later, the Texans had won. Santa Anna surrendered, and Texas was independent.

The Battle of San Jacinto, created by Henry A. McArdle in 1895,
shows the Texan victory over the Mexican Army.

THE LEGEND OF THE ALAMO

The first published account of the Battle of the Alamo appeared in a Texas newspaper on March 24, 1836. Already, the battle was being turned into a legend, or myth. The article was more concerned with celebrating the defenders as noble freedom fighters than with telling the real events. It made the defenders seem like gods. It said their deeds would inspire future generations.

The legend grew with time. The defenders were turned into heroes who had little resemblance to the real men who fought and died at the Alamo. They were larger than life and had performed deeds beyond what any ordinary man could do. The battle and the defenders became symbols of the struggle for liberty shared by all people.

Completed in 1939, this memorial was built on the ground where many people believe the Alamo survivors were put to death by Santa Anna.

By 1841, the Alamo had become so famous that people began to visit it. They drew pictures or took photographs of this symbol of the struggle for liberty.

In 1875, Henry Arthur McArdle became the first artist to show the whole battle in a single painting, *Dawn at the Alamo*. McArdle's painting reflects the legend of the Alamo. The artist wanted to inspire patriotism. He made the defenders look brave and the Mexicans look evil. His painting isn't a correct and fair representation of the battle.

The Alamo legend didn't die in the 1800s but kept growing. Movies made in 1960 and 2004 celebrated the heroes and their fight for freedom.

A fire in 1881 destroyed McArdle's first painting *Dawn at the Alamo*. He completed a second painting with that title in 1905. It now hangs in the Texas Capitol.

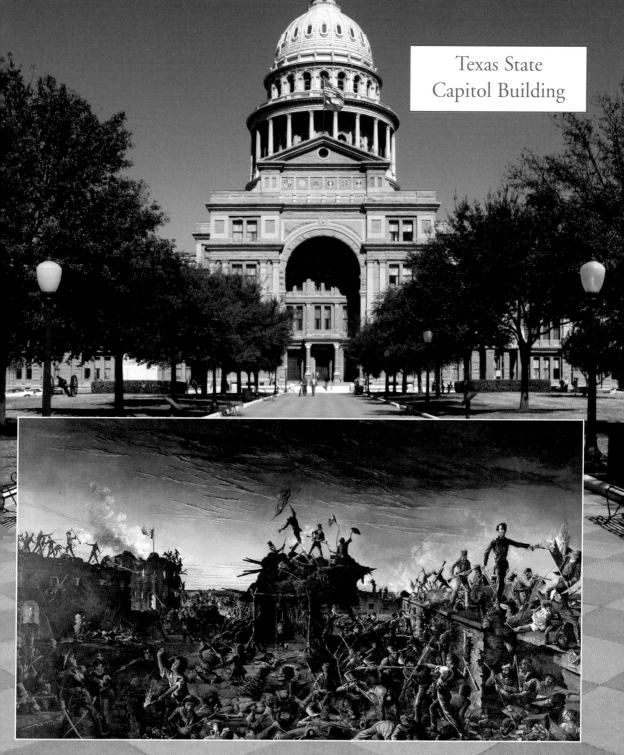

Texas State
Capitol Building

THE ALAMO TODAY

The Battle of the Alamo harmed the mission greatly. Over the years, it was used for many different purposes but wasn't well cared for. Today, though, it has been repaired and is an official historic site, or place. Thousands of people visit every year. You don't have to pay a fee to tour the Alamo, and you can see not only the mission itself but also the historical records and objects kept there. Perhaps someday you'll get to visit the Alamo!

SIEGE AND BATTLE OF THE ALAMO, 1836

February 23	Santa Anna and Mexican soldiers begin siege
February 23–March 6	Mexican soldiers shoot at Alamo; defenders shoot back
February 24	Travis sends letter calling for more volunteers
March 2	Newspaper publishes Travis's letter
March 5	Second newspaper publishes Travis's letter; Alamo defenders run low on ammunition
March 6, 5:00 A.M.	Mexican soldiers attack Alamo
March 6, 6:30 A.M.	Battle of Alamo ends; all defenders dead
March 6	Women, children, and slaves inside Alamo set free

GLOSSARY

ammunition (am-yuh-NIH-shun) Things fired from weapons, such as bullets.

Anglo (ANG-gloh) A white, non-Hispanic person.

defender (dih-FEHN-duhr) Someone who fights to protect something.

dictator (DIHK-tay-tuhr) Someone who holds total power in a country.

frontier (fruhn-TIHR) The edge of a settled country where the wilderness begins.

frontiersman (fruhn-TIHRZ-muhn) A man who lives or works on a frontier.

mission (MIH-shun) A place where church leaders teach their beliefs and help the community.

revolution (reh-vuh-LOO-shun) The overthrow of a government, usually by force.

siege (SEEJ) The use of military power to prevent people and goods from getting into or out of a place.

surrender (suh-REHN-duhr) To give up.

survive (suhr-VYV) To live through.

symbol (SIHM-buhl) An act, object, or person that stands for an idea.

volunteer (vah-luhn-TIHR) Someone who fights in a war but is not a member of the regular army.

INDEX

Due to the changing nature of Internet links, The Rosen Publishing Group, Inc., has developed an online list of Web sites related to the subject of this book. This site is updated regularly. Please use this link to access the list: http://www.rcbmlinks.com/rlr/alamo